What are elephants?

Elephants are the largest land animals in the world. Wild elephants live on the **continents** of Africa and Asia. Elephants are very strong because of their size. Scientists also think that elephants are clever – they have very large brains.

This is an African elephant.

continents Earth's seven big pieces of land.

Trunks, ears, tusks

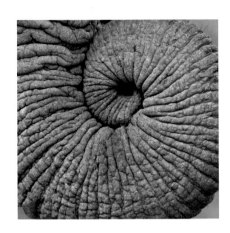

An elephant's trunk is very bendy!

Elephants have a very long nose called a trunk. They use their trunks to hold, eat and smell things. Long teeth called tusks stick out on both sides of the trunk. Elephants have big, floppy ears. An elephant flaps its ears to keep cool when it is hot.

Elephants also use their ears to make themselves look even bigger, to scare away people and other animals.

Big elephants!

Male elephants are called 'bulls'. African bulls can weigh more than 6,000 kilogrammes. Asian bull elephants are smaller, but they can still weigh more than 5,000 kilogrammes. Male elephants are normally bigger than the females. A female elephant is called a 'cow'.

A fully grown elephant can be more than 4 metres tall.

Where elephants live

There are two kinds of African elephants. African bush elephants live on the **savanna**. African forest elephants live in the forest. Asian elephants live on grasslands and in forests in parts of southern Asia.

Asian elephants live where there are lots of green plants to eat.

savanna flat, hot land covered with grass and a few trees.

Elephant food

Elephants are **herbivores**. They use their trunks to pick fruit and leaves from trees. They also eat grass, seeds, bark, twigs and other plants. Sometimes elephants even eat **crops**. Elephants also drink a lot of water – up to 100 litres every day.

Elephants need to eat about 100 kilogrammes of food each day.

herbivores animals that only eat plants.
crops plants that people grow for food.

New elephants

A mother elephant has one calf at a time. A calf is 90 centimetres tall when it is born. Calves drink their mother's milk until they are about three years old. But they also eat plants and other vegetation from three months. Older elephants help keep calves safe from predators such as lions and hyenas. Wild elephants can live for 60 to 80 years.

A mother elephant holds the trunk of her calf so it will stay close to her.

calf a baby elephant.
predators animals that kill and eat other animals.

Elephant families

Elephants live in family groups called herds. The leader of the herd is the oldest female elephant. Herds have 10–20 elephants in them – mostly adult females and young elephants. Adult male elephants like to live alone. The herd spends a lot of time walking around to find food and water. They look after each other and protect sick and young herd members.

An elephant herd may travel a long way to find food and water.

Muddy elephants

Elephants spend time drinking and bathing. They play in the water and mud when it is very hot. They use their trunks to drink and to spray water, mud and dust onto their bodies. The mud stops the Sun from burning their skin – a bit like wearing sunscreen. Their skin is wrinkly and very sensitive. The mud also helps to get rid of any insects on their skin.

Mud and water help elephants to keep cool on a hot day.

Elephants and people

Today, some people go to Africa or Asia to see elephants in the wild. Other people visit zoos to see elephants. It is fun to see these big animals flap their ears and shake their trunks! People also help to protect these animals in the wild. Sadly, some people still hunt and kill these amazing animals, just so that they can sell their **ivory** tusks.

This elephant has broken one of its tusks, but it can grow back.

ivory a hard material (a bit like your teeth) that tusks are made from.

An elephant story

Why is an elephant's trunk so long? A man called Rudyard Kipling wrote a story about this. Long ago, elephants had short noses. A curious young elephant asked a crocodile what he ate for dinner. The crocodile told the elephant to lean in close so that he could tell him. Then the crocodile grabbed the young elephant's trunk and tried to eat him! The crocodile pulled and pulled and the trunk grew longer and longer. That is why elephants have a long trunk!

Useful information

Read More

Saving Wildlife: Grassland Animals & *Saving Wildlife: Rainforest Animals* by Sonya Newland (Franklin Watts, 2014)

Animal Families: Elephants by Tim Harris (Wayland, 2014)

Animal Rescue: Elephant Orphans by Clare Hibbert (Franklin Watts, 2015)

Websites

http://gowild.wwf.org.uk/africa
http://gowild.wwf.org.uk/asia
These WWF sites have African and Asian elephant fact files and a finger puppet activity.

http://animals.nationalgeographic.com/animals/mammals/african-elephant
This site has pictures and videos of African elephants.

Every effort has been made by the Publishers to ensure that these websites are suitable for children, that they are of the highest educational value and that they contain no inappropriate or offensive material. However, because of the nature of the Internet, it is impossible to guarantee that the contents of these sites will not be altered. We strongly advise that Internet access is supervised by a responsible adult.

Index